Samo Kreutz

Forgotten for a Moment

Cyberwit.net
HIG 45 Kaushambi Kunj, Kalindipuram
Allahabad - 211011 (U.P.) India
http://www.cyberwit.net
Tel: +(91) 9415091004
E-mail: info@cyberwit.net

Printed in India at VCORE CONNECT LLP.

*h*andloom …
woven so hastily
her old age

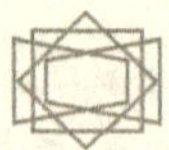

An inner princess

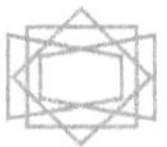

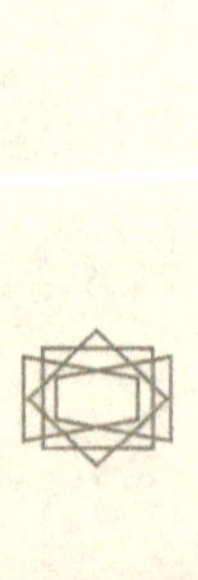

humble shrine
ants are carrying away
the pleas

skromno svetišče
četa mravelj odnaša
sledi priprošenj

young mathematician
ending the pi sequence
morning sunshine

*t*he first time …
a different hug and
a baby's cry

*k*issing
the family dog –
an inner princess

*t*elling her
how lucky she is —
the morning coffee

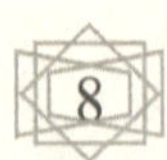

father and son …
their building in a sandbox
not just a castle

long walk
how the sun illuminates
our conversation

hedge maze
making its way
a bird trill

narcissus flower
everywhere around me
grandmother's scent

without a mask …
so much different
this butterfly

vast meadow
freshly greened
grasses and my hope

*p*lanting …
already germinated
a child in him

*w*hite daffodils
more sweet-smelling
daydreams

*s*eeding season
promptly multiplied
the presence of sparrows

*s*orrel leaf …
ending in his mouth
an ant track

*l*ettuce seedlings
no more on a bare ground
her shadow

*p*lanting beans
a small child speaks
about the cosmos

*r*iverbank
she pours into the water
a loud laughter

*o*ne-hour drive …
no closer to the end
of bird song

*b*usy street …
breaking the rules
a small leaf

*ac*cident repair centre …
almost as new
a beetle

*p*etrol station
I fill up my fuel tank
with bird sounds

*ch*oosing a tenant
first one to arrive
a bumblebee

young courier
the postal package
full of smiles

*t*heir tryst
he brings nothing
but a ladybug

*b*ouquet of roses
even more appealing
his smile

*f*irst amendment
finally in unison
barking and chirping

*p*ond water
all these lives
within

*t*hrowing pebbles
I count the splashes
of her joy

*f*ragrant flower
attracting the bees
even his shadow

*A*pril fool's day
adorned with primroses' scent
the stable

*a*pple blossoms
the moment of silence
after the explosion

*e*mbracing
the places he used to seat –
this plum tree

*h*er eyes
when she smiled –
two daffodils

*w*ildlife park …
in a kangaroo's pouch
my lullaby

*a*lmost dark …
looking for the keys
she finds a word

*h*uge crow   *o*gromna vrana
carefully protected   na mokri travi straži
the child's cap   otroško kapo

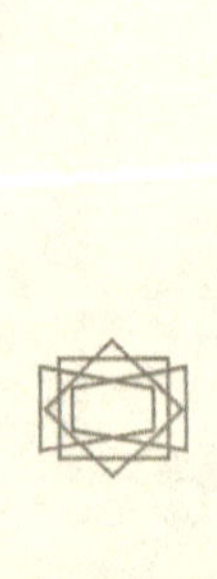

Coming as a friend

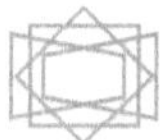

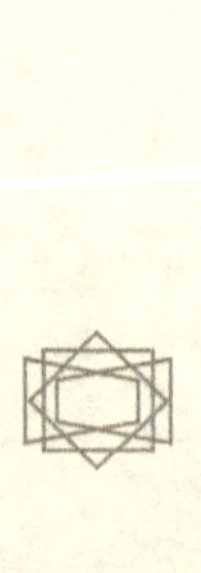

*u*ncovered buds
the climbing rose seduces
a bumblebee swarm

*r*azkriti popki
roj čmrljev zapeljuje
roža vzpenjavka

*f*lirty girl
winking back at her
the morning sun

*b*itter cry
great grandma's lap
too different

*w*orker bee
nourished with pollen
the child in me

*B*loomsday …
already Leopold Bloom
this little boy

yellow iris …
his promise to get married
to the granny

peonies …
all the beauty
of her eyes

shrub roses
talking to them
talking to father

*m*arathon
unregistered contestant
a plum blossom

*s*oft summer grass …
the years I knew how to fall
properly

*v*acation
in the funny papers
a siren wail

*s*unny day
my father watches me –
not with his eyes

*h*undred ways
to express love –
a dog

truce …
all the fallen
blossoms

*c*onnecting
one flower to another –
the trail of ants

*b*irthday toast
filled with sunshine
her glass

*t*ropical heat
a sweaty tourist occupies
the pigeon's shadow

*o*cean waves
the foam swallows
my voice

*s*afari
traveling around in a jeep
baobab's tree leaf

*t*raditional shrine
all the languages
of a statue

linguistic barrier ...
that hand communication
with a wasp

drought season
coming as a friend
the sun in boy's eyes

spiritual dancing
the special moves
of the fire

*en*camping …
forgotten for a moment
his demolished house

*a*ncient ruins
visiting them briefly
a children's song

*s*weltering heat
even a bell sound
rests

watering the roses
the way she caressed
my hair

wildfire …
the uncertain moments
after his revelation

dirty laundry
full of greasy stains
an old man's shadow

summertime …
flushing the toilet
flushing the rainbow

pee puddle
even the sun in it
different

open door church …
at the Christ's right hand
a stray puppy

basket of penny buns
a guest in my home
the slug

ripening grain …
how quickly we became
adults

open-air concert
the prima donna's voice
jasmine scented

*e*verything
he loved about her –
a pink hibiscus

*d*andelion wreath
visible from afar –
a headstone

*t*ouching
her husband's shiny face
a carnation on the grave

quiet evening
still roaring in him
the rejection

end of the summer …
just the right size for a wind
her thong

resting hours
not even a bit tired
the purr

*b*edtime drink
he takes one last sip
of the granny's tale

*f*alling off the bike
a boy finds in the grass
a smile

*p*adec s kolesa
sredi bohotne trave
dečkov nasmešek

Unmeasured depth

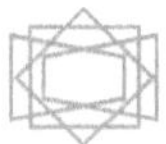

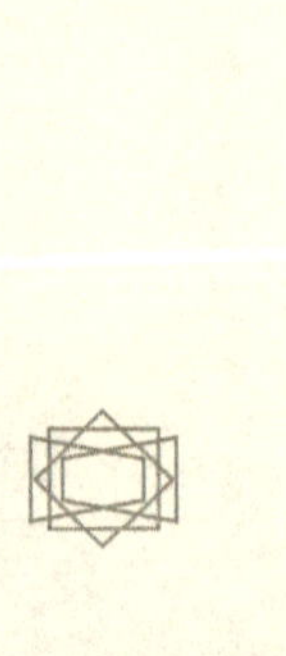

*r*enovated house
clothing donation bin
eliminated

*p*reurejen blok
siv zabojnik Humane
tokrat umaknjen

*n*ew sunrise
as if everything were
so simple

headwaters …
flowing forcefully
a newborn's cry

childhood
an unmeasured depth
of this ocean

first visit
her great grandson's cry
much more tangible

*i*magining
a small boy imagining
me as an old man

*o*bserved …
his broad smile
in a dog's eyes

*e*nergy saving …
not as hot as usual
their date

wedding
whatever might follow –
the blank canvas

his third wife
that childhood swear
not to have a girlfriend

autumn forest
the changed colour
of her voice

old cherry tree
concealed in the crown
my youth

waterfall …
the abrupt urge to share
his problems

camping
all the snugness
of the autumn woods

*b*ackyard …
fallen birch tree leaf
a wheelchair user

*h*er photo
still so attractive –
to the mosquito

*b*ullet train
rushing across the state
a barberry shrub scent

*p*ilgrimage …
a faithful companion –
the juicy apple

*s*mell of petunias
hunched underneath
Jesus on the cross

*a*utumn pasture
abundantly feasted
our eyes

*p*lane in the air
going to a distant city
my loneliness

*c*older days …
under additional clothes
the viruses

*s*trong wind
the roast beef smell
on her necklace

*c*loudy sky
a different look
of his father

a talk
at the porch –
midday rain

*d*ownpour …
a massive pond filled
with yellow leaves

*c*lothesline
forgotten on it
a wet sparrow

*s*hortage …
an old crossword puzzle
freshly solved

*f*orty days rain
drenched to the bone
a menopause

*f*ence
inside his neat home
a floodwater

*o*ld sandpit
a time when the rain was still
a playful companion

*s*queaky floor
much closer to me
sundown

a brick
from the Berlin Wall –
her job search

*s*wallows migration …
he passes on to children
his dad's memories

*t*he warmth
of my granny's hands –
a soil after the harvest

so frisky …
the autumn breeze
in the grave flowers

*h*is absence …
showing me the house
this moth

*n*apping cat
that desire to rest
all my worries

*n*ightfall …
the whispered words
in her doll's ear

*b*lue moon
finally emerged
his wisdom tooth

*c*ampfire …
I take another sip
of storyteller's shadow

*h*umankind …
before and after
the starry night

*s*mall beer garden
occupying a table for two
the ice crust

*m*anjši letni vrt
mizo za dva zaseda
skorjica ledu

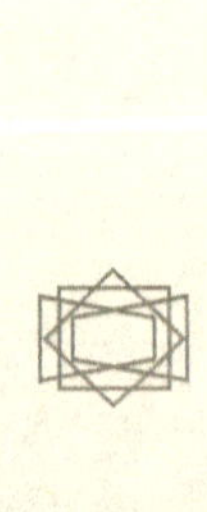

The prospect of warmth

snow everywhere
the only cleared path –
to the cemetery

celec vseokrog
edina sčiščena pot –
k pokopališču

heavy fog …
that exhausting search
for a crane-operator

jogging …
still not outran
the past

high rent prices
his shadow tenants
my pocket

big discount
on the shelves for sale
an empty space

*o*live oil
those calloused hands
of a Greek huckster

*a*uction …
not sold to anyone
the crow's shriek

*g*asoline shortage
grandfather stays
in his youth

bird feather
that long arm
of my shadow

postelection day
outside the parliament
food odour

traffic light
waiting for a green signal
the storm cloud

*a*bandoned meadow
unaware of hidden mines
the breeze

*l*ooking
and still looking in the sky
a war refugee

*d*ecember downpour
the countless ways to be
wrong

*f*ortune teller
ending her sentences
a shrieky magpie

*h*ailstorm …
in a retirement home
all the fragrances

*a*fter the rain
connected to the network
computer and the sun

*i*ce cold day …
the prospect of warmth
male bonding

*s*carecrow …
all the chased birds
in my eyes

*c*old hands …
the touches that remain
on her body

red signal
just enough time to talk
about his illness

ice pellets
filled with coldness
even these words

chemotherapy …
embracing her tightly
a gull's shriek

my breath
that delicacy
of snowflakes

*f*ading light
granddaughter describes
the photos in his album

*t*all cupboard …
grabbing the cookie jar
a moonlight

*o*ld kitchen
dripping into the sink
the sound of a clock

*f*orgotten jubilee
his standard excuses –
the wind from graveyard

*r*ough sea …
entangled in plastic
her ashes

*a*wake
when she sleeps –
a husband's photo

*c*ultural holiday
artwork in front of me –
a snowy grove

*k*ulturni praznik
umetnina pred menoj –
zasnežen gozdič

A WORD OR TWO ABOUT THE AUTHOR

Samo Kreutz lives in Ljubljana, Slovenia. He began to write as an eight-year-old boy, when he wrote his first story (and later a poem). One day his parents told him that simply by writing he cannot earn enough for a decent life, so he replied that he will become a writer and a joiner. Now, at the age of forty-eight, he is not yet a joiner (nor a carpenter), but the Bachelor of Economics, who besides poetry and short stories, also writes novels and haiku (since 2011). He is the author of ten books in Slovene (all published by the Ekslibris, publishing house in Ljubljana) and three in English (they are haiku books; one is titled *The Stars for Tonight*, the second is *A Time Different from Ours*, and the last *No Bigger Than a Crumb*, all published by Cyberwit.net). His work has appeared in various Slovenian literary magazines, anthologies, on national Radio, on several international websites, e- and printed journals (most recently in the *Autumn Moon Haiku Journal*, and in the *Lothlorien Poetry Journal*).

A NOTE ABOUT THE BOOK

Forgotten for a Moment consists of 155 haiku. The poems in this collection are about our lives (and everything, what marks them, but we are simply choosing to forget it). They are joined by those with a touch of nature, so that new meanings or new contrasts could be established. The majority of these haiku can be found (in English, Slovene or both versions) in printed journals: *Better Than Starbucks: Poetry and Fiction Journal, Kingfisher Journal, Lothlorien Poetry Journal, Seashores: Haiku Journal,* and *Taj Mahal Review,* on websites: *Akita International Haiku Network, Ariel Chart: international literary journal, Asahi Haikuist Network, Autumn Moon Haiku Journal, Cattails: A Journal of the United Haiku and Tanka Society, Cold Moon Journal, Creatrix Haiku and Poetry Journal, First Literary Review – East, Green Ink Poetry, Ink Sweat & Tears: The poetry and prose webzine, Jalmurra: Art and Poetry Journal, Locutio, Poetry Pea, Stardust Haiku Online Journal, The Bamboo Hut, The Big Windows Review, The Haiku Foundation (Haiku Dialogue), The Heron's Nest,* and *Wales Haiku Journal,* in anthologies: *Haiku zbornik: Ludbreg, Pesem si: zbornik, Samoborski haiku susreti Darko Plažanin,* and in quite a few broadcasts on the national Radio.

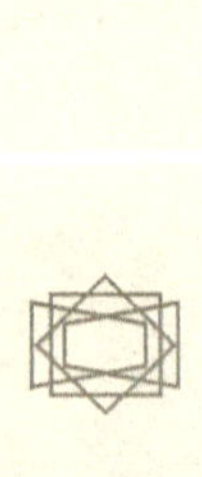

CONTENTS

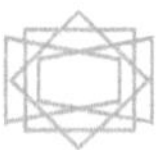

www.ingramcontent.com/pod-product-compliance
Lightning Source LLC
LaVergne TN
LVHW051504170726
843492LV00002B/799